Wind

Aryrejin El

Dedicated to EL

AUTHORS NOTE

I have always loved stories.
Faerie tales and folk lore and history of all kinds.
Poetry which falls from my mouth unbidden and unrestrained.
I admire how unique and similar each and every one of us are.
How we read the same words, share the same heart ache,
and yet, in the end, have taken a path different
from anyone else. I want you to find something
in these words of mine, unique only to you.

Fill up the pages. Dog ear the corners. Live in this book.
Scribble notes and poems of your own making in the blank spaces.
Explode upon the page with colors (I recommend pencil).
Let it be a refuge. Let it remind you the world is still a beautiful place to
sing of. Words you come back to again and again to remember no one
is alone in their growth and the finding of their path.

Come and sit with me for a while.

Aryrejin El April 2022

HEARTBREAK

HOW RARE THE MOON

How rare the moon,
Fades from the sky,
It sits in my hand, and the stars are alone.
How rare the moon,
Keeping me close at night
I beckon it down; we laugh with delight.
How rare the moon,
Wishes me to dance,
I sing it my songs; he claps his hands.
How often the sun
Has burned my skin too deep.
I want to be free, I want to be free
Only the sky knows what I seek.
Only the forest gives me relief.
Have you not seen my eyes so white;
See in your soul and hold on tight.
Are you, are you singing to me
Or is it my voice I listen for?

You
Held the sun in
Your gaze
I held you in my arms
Yet like the wind you shift
And like the sun I fade

THE BOY BY THE TRAIN

There's a boy by the train.
I see him.
His eyes seem pale and vivid,
He is waiting.
I don't know who for, no one does.
He comes here every day to wait.
Stands at the base of the tracks,
Feet barely touching the warm metal.
This boy is old.
He has been here for centuries.
Waiting.
Maybe he doesn't wait.
Maybe I just think that to make myself feel better.
To have some justification for not speaking to him.
He wouldn't want to talk to me,
No one does.
I was pulled on in the womb,
Ready for leaving on wings I never got to use.
I am scraggly and tall and a hopeless romantic when it comes to love.
That is why I think he waits.
Oh, place no judge,
You think the same.
The reason why this boy waits all day.
We all have our inward thinkings.
The thoughts no one sees.
We are no different.
But he sees,
With his vivid eyes he knows we look at him.
And it frightens us with thoughts of love.
That is why he waits.
To place the blame he knows must come.
But this is another of my inward thoughts.
There's a boy by the train.
I don't talk to him.
I'm too shy to speak.
He loves me now, this I know.
For just last week he stood his eyes on my freckled face
And a smile so thin and hard,
Made me think he didn't smile at all,
But he did.

It is love now that I feel.
He has brought the thoughts to life.
My father has banned me from going to him.
And why should he not?
This boy is known renown as the
Train Ghost.
The one who swallows the souls of lost passengers.
But this is more judging.
He smiled again this morning. The boy.
By the train.
His hair is white like winter fluff,
But it makes me think of dandelions all aglow.
His skin is light and dark,
He doesn't seem to have a shape
But shifts in and out of sight.
This is it.
I have done it. I have gone up and said,
"Hello."
A sideways glance.
A silent laugh.
You startled me, his eyes seem to say.
But his face stays the same.
I try again the next day.
Hello.
Hello.
There's a boy by the train.
"I need to speak with you."
I finally say.
"Why do you stand here all day?"
He shakes his head, then looks at me.
And the sight in his eyes is more than I could see.
A sadness beyond disbelief.
His voice is low
And hollow. I don't think I hear it at all.
But I do.
"If your love was in the past,
And you could return to her,
Wouldn't you?"
His voice, one I'll never forget,
broke my heart so no one could mend it.
Then he is gone.
Lost in the crowds of street walkers.

Lost in a sea of on lookers.
There's a girl by the train…

Sometimes
I wonder
What the world would be like
If I had never met you

Maybe you think of me
Maybe I'm someone close in your mind
But I am so afraid
That you do not know my name
That I'm a stranger to you
That you won't wait for me
That you'll forget
Your promise
Please
Prove me wrong

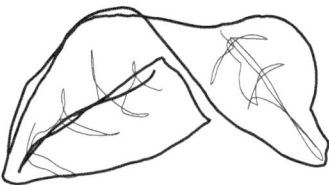

BETWEEN

Between the mountains
Between the moon, between the daylight
Between the dunes.
Between the near
And between the far.
It is my love I'm searching for. With this sword upon my head. With this
crown between my hands.
Fiercely
Riding out the storms- now I'm weary and I'm torn.
Between the throne
And between the door
Leaving my robes on the floor.
Running once more to the glen.
It is your heart I must defend.
Between the now
And between the then
How could you not comprehend!
Throwing roses to the sky, I'm bare and wild and at your side.
Now there is no space nor any time to tell how
Your love changed my life.
Even from this throne, I still can hear the golden
Laughter of our years.

I've
Fought against
A raging storm
I've
Left the broken-hearted
War
I held you on those summer days
How could
I
Have known you'd
Fly away

They told me
Time would mend these open wounds.
But if Time was on my side
I'd still have you
Beside me.

THE ROSES COLORS

Oh, my dear, I'd pluck you a rose
If I knew the colors of your heart
Oh, my dear, I'd pluck you a rose
The dearest rose by far.
Oh, my dust, I'd weave you the stars
Weave them into your wings
Then up you'd fly with the rustless stars and far away from me.

Yet I'd rush in the battlefield
Without a sword or bow
And I'd wage war on all the kings
If you had told me so.

Oh, my dear, I'd give you the sea
But that is where your heart lies
And on at night along with my cries
I hear your empty passed sighs.

Yet I'd rush in the battlefield
With just a book in hand
And I'd wage war on all the kings
And offer up the land.

Yet, oh, my rose,
Your thorns prick deep
For I can no longer stand.

Oh, my love, I'd plant you a rose
For the dearest rose by far.
Oh, my love, I'd plant you a rose
If I had not taken this arrow to heart.

REMEMBRANCE

Do you remember, what you used to say?
You'd say, darling, my sweetheart, lets love just this way.
Do you remember, how we used to feel?
We'd whisper sweet wish words in each other's ears.
Dandelion fluff settles in your hair, as I told you my secrets stolen away
by summer's air.
And have you forgotten, what I used to sing?
That our love is greater than sunlight on angels' wings.
Sunlight on angels' wings.
Sunlight. Angel wings.

My love, I'm still waiting. It's cold in my bed.
My love I still listen. The trees speak your name.
My darling the wind torments me with your sounds.
Of love.

I still remember, where we used to go.
No path, uncharted, we led the way.
I still remember, how you used to sway.
Rocked by the wind. Changed by the waves.
You used to tell me; love, take my hand. Feel the earth move, every
grain of sand.
And I've not forgotten how we used to play.
The world was our plaything, life was a game.
Life was a game to you.
To me.

My love I still see you. Your eyes fill my sight.
My love I still feel you. Your arms holding tight.
Your breath when its day. Your warmth when its night.
I still feel you.
My darling I'll always love you.

The difference between
Heartbreak
And
Heartache
Is that a break will mend
While an ache will go on throbbing

You held
Life
In your hands
Why
Throw that away

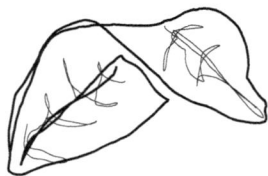

SURVIVAL

I longed for you that night your tears hit the floor. When you felt so empty.
I prayed.
But you wouldn't take my call, I doubt you even looked at your phone.
'-You don't get to be heart broken,' you'd said, 'for things you never took a chance on.'
But even you will not take a lick of your own advice.
I never knew the pain of absence, until I could no longer say your name.
You said that life was too much- and then never enough.
Was it really so hard?
Were there never smiles, never laughter? No sunrises worth seeing? No stars worth waiting through the night to see how they changed?
Was the joy I gave not enough? Was the joy I received in return so worthless?
Do you hold yourself so low that life isn't something you can obtain?
Why? Why.
Why not sleep and try again? Why not give yourself a chance to survive?
To thrive.
Look, maybe you'll never read this, maybe all these words seem point-less to you. Or perhaps you could give me a chance, hear me out.
I want you to survive.
I want you to have the best life possible, no matter who you are, or what you've done.
I want you to live.
(I don't know if these words will reach you, or if you'll let them matter enough to change anything.)
AWHYAWA I open my heart, the love You've placed there, to the beautiful beings You created.
Please, survive, I swear there is something better out there.
There is a difference only you can make, believe me, I know doubt too.
There is life worth living in this broken world.
There is a place where we can be free.
But it doesn't lie in death.
It lies in the true, everlasting, always standing, love of the Most High.
-reach out. ask HIM to be someone you may stand with.

I am a little China doll
My tears hid behind
Pale paint and make up

Glass fingers and
Glass toes
Could I be more than glass?
Could I be made of light?

SOMEONE

I
Think
I
Lost someone once.
Someone dear to me.

I know I did.
I can feel it in my bones.
An emptiness
A longing
A hollow sound where my soul used to be.
My sword glows in faded light.
A cry rips from me.
They have taken out my heart, replacing it with an alien.
A voice.
A feeling.
I cannot help but long for her return.
I have been away so long…

I think I
Lost someone once.
Not that it matters now,
I won't remember her.
Not that I can't.
Her figure comes to me in shadows,
Guiding me through an eclipse of despair.
A forest of nothing.
Her mouth.
Her neck. Her jaw.
She tempts me!
Her scent.
Sweet.
Tangy.
Used to suffocate me, now
I am intoxicated.
I walk empty streets. She is never beside me.
I feel her laugh.

I know I lost someone.

Once.
Would she recognize me now?
This face I've donned is unfamiliar to her.
My hands no longer hold the passion they once did.
I speak so hopelessly!
How can you not understand?
I am a man in suffering.
How can you leave me?
Every time I walk these steps,
Steps that she and I once took,
I feel a sense of longing and desire.
Rivers and trees now fill our hollowed footsteps.
The lives I pass by
The people who see me, the eyes I know
All look the same now.
She saw different.

I have lost.
I feel her though
Inside me.
Her sound deeply impacts my soul.

ARLAIN

I guess this is it
My world laid out before me
I guess this is it
Time wound up in circles
But I'm not giving up
Arlain
Though we'll never be the same again
No
We'll never be the same
Are you there
Arlain
I've given everything for you
The world now is dark
Your light is gone
Beautiful Arlain
Blissful Arlain
Did you have to go so soon
You know I fight the dark to find you
You know the light is yours to wield
But you don't have to fight
I'll be your shield
I know your name
Arlain
It is a song on my tongue
Let's run into the light
Before the dark destroys what we hold
I'm not giving up
Arlain
Though our hearts won't speak the same
After this

Why hold on to this fear?
It only
weighs
you
down

It was dark once
Now there is light
My soul sought for something
Now I have rest

Tendrils of spider webs glow in the faded sun
I am alone in this forest
I am breaking
Hope
Hopelessness
I forgot what this felt like
To love someone and watch them leave
To be waiting
to be looking for them
despite the realization
that they no longer walk this world
No

I am in pain yes
I am broken hearted yes
But I refuse to believe the irony of
Hopelessness
I am held

I will seek healing no matter what
I will remember I held your hand
I will remember I kissed you
That we sang the same language that early summers day
This will be enough for me to remember you well

HOPE

The wind speaks to me through the sways
and groanings of the trees.
I have always been wild.
I have always been free.
Now I reach out for you.
Now voices join my song.
I have never been alone-
And neither have you.

Lately,
I haven't been able to sleep.
But I watch the stars
And think of you
And the hours are not wasted.

Do not
Fear the dark
My friend
Step over it

Hang on to the
Joy
It's the only way
We will make it in
This world

It was only a
single moment
that I knew
you
but I've
loved you
ever since

I'll
Write a hundred letters
To the one I love
I'll leave them
In a dust covered box
I'll
Recite them here
Beneath the tree we sang of
In that long ago song
I
Won't let go of you
Not till the day I die

STREETLAMP

Streetlamp. Cherry trees. An angel who lost her wings.
But what do I know of such things?
I am just a June day in an April summer.
Waiting for a love that never came on a spring morn,
when snow still touched the ground.
Winter loss.
Park bench. Shaded rivers. Leave me in a forest 'till dawn.
But do not hurt my heart.
For I am just a starless night with no clouds to shade my mood.
I wait still.
My love came, a July dame on his arm.
I saw her dark skin and flashing eyes.
The heat of her stare.
Are you truly? Or are you a fool?
I am a fool.
July came and went. My love is alone again. How are you so sad?
Rise and riser still.
Someday you will see
The white of my own eyes.
And you will know then that I have been waiting centuries to meet you.
Perhaps we met before?
London town. Empty floor. A babe who would not come.
Perhaps we met before… long ago.
Perhaps you are waiting too?
Gown of curling blue. Red hair that would not cut.
A fear. A smile.
Hope.
Streetlamp.
I am back again.
Light eyes. Dark crown. A smile to wash the worry
-is how I feel for you.
You are Green. Brown. White. Blue. Hazel.
Cool.
You are water. Your eyes ever shifting in the sun.
Pink petals rain a winter night.
We stare at stars. Eat their light.
You are not a man prone to fright.
So why have we not met?
Streetlamp.
It grows dark and light.

I am in and out of dreams you and I share.
Come love. Come.
I wait a while still.

You know you've found the
Right one
When they do not
Overlook
Your flaws but
Accept them

LOVE

It's the tiny moments I remember.
The little stuff.
The written prayers that continue to make me smile.
The peace I suddenly feel when I see you.
I'm glad there was no white horse.
No roses.
No love songs.

I'm glad all it took for me to love you was that odd conversation we had.
That moment when suddenly I wasn't afraid of what you might mean
to me. Of how that might change me.
I cannot say the words 'I love you' for they have lost their meaning in
this world.

I do not want an undying love.
I want an everlasting, always standing, constantly singing, type of love.
A love that is firm in the storms, unbreakable.
A love where we sit and marvel at the sky together.
Where hand-picked herbs and dried flowers make everything better.
Where we can truly be free with each other.
I just want you beside me. No matter what happens.
Always.

Right now…
I don't know what to tell you.
Honestly, I'm stalling.
Giving you a chance to say something. To tell me anything, really.
Just hearing you speak is like a song going off in my head, and I don't
even know your name.
You're so deeply intwined in my soul-
I'm terrified
And ecstatic
And full of joy.
You fill me completely with a deep-hearted peace.
And I don't even know your name…

I know love has a sound.
Yet its not birds or waterfalls or star songs.
Though somedays I would like it to be.
I don't think love sounds like anything,
Or else the world would be full of music.
And it isn't. At least, not the songs we should be singing.
Though, I know that love is not quiet.
There is a look in ones eye that comes with love.
True love.
Pure, unrelenting, determination.
One that says-
I am going to be here for you no matter what.
I am going to fight your demons and restore you from all pain.
I will be there on the bad days, and on the good.
I will be here for you.
That is the kind of song love is singing.

The air had never known such beauty
As the day the trees flew
Roots dangling beneath them
Dirt and stone dropping from their grasp
Higher and higher they flew
Never knowing how the depths of time held them down
And they sang

For a moment
I became part of the forest
My knees have sunk into the earth
My eyes reach for the sky and my hand follows
The sounds of birds
Of sunlight
Of wind
Flit near me, rushing to consume me
My voice is joyous at their sounds
I am a part of this world
Of this earth
I am a root
A leaf
A cry of wind
A bud waiting
I am something else entirely
I am free

I Wish only to
Exist
In the light of the
Setting sun

To love is
Endurance
Strength
Vitality

I wish only to
Be

I want to find the sun
I want to know where it sets
To follow the line of light as it fades
As it rises
I want to see the first shine of
Hope
As the dawn breaks
Grant me this one happiness and I shall live for a
Thousand lives

I keep my life in a book
My soul
The song in which it is written

I'm praying for you softly.
Quiet.
In my own head.
I remember the summer where you laughed as I cried, then took my
hand.
I remember the moment our song touched the sky.
I cling to these; memories I almost feel I have stolen.
I have known you forever now,
Minus an hour.
Sure, this prayer is almost silent
Buts it's the loudest I can muster.
Sometimes, I don't have words to tell you my story,
terrified you won't care.
Yet here you are.

GLASS HEART

It was a glass heart you broke
But you never knew it
You thought I was steel
I was metal
You never expected me to be someone as fragile
As paper
But I am
I heal myself over and over and now the warrior is tired
I'm tired of running and moving without
Grace
I am a dancer
You will know my song I sing it loudly enough
I have known loss
I have known gain
Underneath my crown is a weight that is light
I am not glass
I have risen above that existence
To become more than a see through heart on a string

FLIGHT

STAY

Take my hand
Don't fly away
Hear my song, asking you to stay
Though the wind is crying
Howling with a thousand
Words
Won't you stay for me
Won't you stay with me
Long are the nights
When you're far from my heart
Yet here in my arms
I am holding a shell of who you are
Though I know this path is hard to bear
There's so much beauty in its light
In the sounds we share
Won't you stay for me
Won't you stay with me
They say to love as the
River does
Ebbing out to the sea
Yet our love is stronger
As the day and the night
As the sea and the sun so are we
And I would give up
A thousand stars
Just to be right where you are
Won't you stay for me
Won't you stay with me

The grass
The wind
Your breath
All lift me up and settle
In my
Chest

We are tethered to this world
Like trees
Waiting to be lifted up
And fly into the
Beyond
Encircled
by the wind

My eyes are drawn to the
Sun
The lights of the
Sky
And the depths of the
Woods
Oh, what I would give to
Breathe
A wilder
Air

My hands are speckled with color
A starry horizon
A land of many suns
Appears beneath my hands
I want to know what it feels like
To create
To tell a story with colors and form- or lack of
To feel free with a single tilt of my wrist
A flick of my eyes
As I choose among the many the
One color to be born

FLIGHT

There is a field of yellow winged moths.
Sucking the sweet, life-giving nectar from purple clovers and many
petaled pale flowers.
I'm sure it must be wonderful. To live as a winged one.
Carefree and happy and blissful—
Is how I picture it.
But I never could imagine it.
The instinctual drive to eat, to live and create new life.
The predators of sky and earth always lurking.
Always waiting for you to flit near.
The constant flight from rain and snow and motor vehicles
which merely speed past fields such as these.
(I know I once did. Before I learned to see.)
The shelter one must seek before the storms.
The weight of the wings must be lighter than air.
Yet heavy enough to topple trees when in multitude.
No, I never could exist as one of them, I don't know if I'd have the
strength.
But I cherish their life,
As small as it may be.

She's the kind of girl
Who carries
Moths with broken wings
To refuge
And breaks for
Butterflies

To believe that your life starts out small,
Is a lie.
You are grander than the mountains.
As fierce as the sea.
This world would have you turn your head to look in its mirror.
Telling you
That you are nothing.
I loved you before the stars were born.
I hold your name in My hand and whisper out your story.
Come.
Let Me show you who you are.

I fall into the
Deep
I lose myself in an ocean
Of stillness
Yet I cannot hold
Back this tide
I will not
Control
This storm

Some days
I believe the lies that I am
Fragile.
That I am made of glass.
Not to be touched less I am
Marred.
But then
You never could deny me
My truth

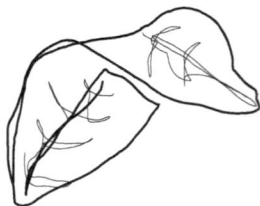

She is not a girl of
Lightning
Not a girl who turns her enemies to
Dust
But a girl who sets forth to
Heal

Do not deny yourself
Who you are
For the sake of what
Other people
May think

RIVER BEND

My hair is bound
Tied back and tight
I've waited too long
I pull at strings, at constrictions, at the lies they told
The river purls, washing away my reliance on fear
My arms raise, bringing the sky closer
My hips sway in the tall grass, my feet move slowly
Unsure which direction they shall take
The wind pulls at me, its grip secure
I'm not ready to fly
I dig my feet into the ground, steady my breath. The water surges
I must learn myself first before anyone else knows me
I must remember who I am
The water consumes me
There, in the dark of the depths
A tiny light is ready to take flight

They told me to stop when the
Sun set
That my voice was too loud for the
Dark
I refuse to be
Silent

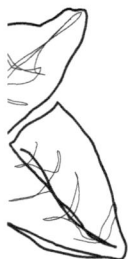

Do not think
My fire
Is naught but
Ash and wind
I'm merely renewing the
Flame

They whispered to her,
Taunting
Jeering

Their words harsh and grinding
You will not withstand our thunder
You will not trouble our armies
You will not battle against our great storms

She listened
Heard the words, understood their meaning
Saw her enemies with white, pale eyes
Glowing through the dark
She replied
A wild grin across her face
Your storm is of no trouble to me

There is only one fight I'd put on armor for.
Only one war cry worth my time.
To see your joy again is my greatest wish.
To see you smile.
To see you free.

The fire of your heart was what I fought for.
The light in your eyes as you gazed at me.
A soldier come back from war.
No more words to say, but you spoke for me.
It's all right now.
There's peace.
And you held me as I tried to pour out my sorrow.
There wasn't any moon that night, the sun too low for anything but
different shades of blue.
I couldn't see your tears; you couldn't see my cracks.
It's been too many years to count, but this is the closest thing I have to
truth.
The sun lit dawn I never saw.
All I remember is your light.
Your color as it poured into my life.
Lighting up my darker half.

I must
Admit, I'm living this
Moment as if its
One
I could
Live again.

Thank you for
Waking me.
-Life

I didn't realize
The world was this crazy
Outside my walls
And doors
Windows only for peeking
I didn't realize
The extent of
Help
We need

At least now I have
My purpose

RESILIENCE

I used to know the path I wanted,
The journey I was on.

I envy those who are but a speck in the ocean,
Who have no worry of
Waves or tides
But drift endlessly
When I wanted to be the ocean itself.

I envy those who plan every detail,
Know every end
Every possibility
Who lay their path out for the world to follow.
But I could never be like them.

As I lay here, remembering
Those who tried to crush my heart in their hands
Yet came away with splinters of glass,
I laugh.
For I know better.

Deep within me I have questioned the world
This is the bravest thing you can do,
To question everything you know.
This quest for truth and alignment.

I know the path I seek is nowhere to be found-
For I must forge it.
And when I get up
I'll run
Towards a horizon brighter than the sun.

But for now I'll rest
Watching the stars
Waiting for dawn to come once more,
This dark never could hold me for long.
-resilient

 FAITH

One raindrop can lift the sea
What can I do

You are so critical of yourself
When I find you
Beautiful

I have
Never
Gazed at an ocean
And not thought of
You
The foundations of the
Earth
Could not sway me
I run when I hear
Your voice

The heat of Your heart
The depth of Your love
Even the stars
Are dim next to
Your fire

Holy
Is the ground you walk on
For holy is Your Name
Oh, my Love
The stars sing of You
The trees whisper and chime out Your Name
Come
And let me know You
Let me too sing as best I can
Of Your Mighty
And holy grace
You are the only infinite Love I have known
You surpass all
You have not broken my heart
Or left me alone

ENTRUSTED

The moon shines above
Reflected by the light in your eyes
The trees whisper words
Words to make you laugh all the time
Your sun-kissed lips
Are softer than the sea could ever be
Yet the words that they produce are stronger than the waves

Oh how I long to tell you
That with every passing day my heart
Has grown to be so much more of yours than mine

The grass parts beneath your feet as you walk on holy ground
And my darling your smile is greater than the stars
And when you sleep
It's like watching an angel sing
Upon a summer's morning you arise

Oh how I long to tell you
That with every passing day my heart
Has grown to be so much more of yours than mine
Please don't reject it- It's the only one I've got
My heart is yours.

You are
Water
To my
Soul
Light to my
Shadows
You
Love
Are the Only One
To contain me-
Make me whole

Do not take my heart from me
For it is too large to carry.
Do not steal my sight,
For my eyes are sunlight
Burning through the fog.
Do not take my hands,
For they dance as much as my feet.
My soul is wild
And I am free.
No one can take my
Life
From me.

RELEASE

I'm running.
Yearning to lift off the ground.
But the force of my will is not enough to free me.
Gravity holds.
I sit in a cage, bars of metal and old weeds
which once were the flowers of spring.

The thralls of summer hold my heart,
yet winter is in my hands.
The land is warm as I sit and freeze.
The sky gray, holding thresholds of blue.

I love this earth which encases me when sorrow is too much.
The ground holds my memories and the sky my laughter.
You have caught me in a jar and poured my soul onto the page.

I am liquid, water rippling under your breath.
I am a sound not yet heard, yet you know my voice.
I could sing you a thousand songs, compose a hundred poems,
yet I will never be able to convey my hope in you.
The life you have given me.

I am a
Bird
AWHYAWA
My home
My tree
I am a
Bloom
Waiting to open
AWHYAWA
My roots and leaves
The stem of my
Life
I do not know what to
Tell you
Those who have never seen
AWHYAWA
Is my
All
As much as my
King

I feel
Your
Heart
Through my
Fingertips

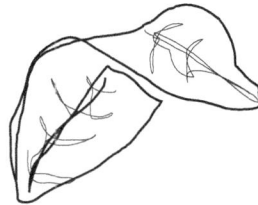

The waters of the world are
At my fingertips
The
Life of all things

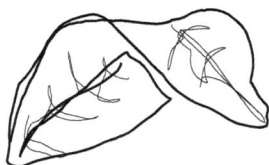

There was only
Your
Voice
Before the dark
Only Your
Sounds

COME AND KNOW

Oh, Love.
For once I have nothing to say.
There are no words to express my feelings.
No metaphors which could convey how.
I am…
With You.
In every moment of my life, I am with You.
I sit beside You, I sing with You, I dance and make You laugh.
You pull me into Your arms,
telling me I am whole,
made brighter than the stars.

Oh, Love.
How can I explain to them?
How can I tell them of Your beautiful Love,
when they are blind to it?

Oh, Love.
It makes my heart ache to think of those who do not see You as I do,
who have had no sight.
Those who are blinded by their own eyes.
But You see, my Love.
You know their pain, but they do not turn to You
for safety, for peace, for love.
They come demanding answers,
relief for the same pain they caused You with their hate.
Their hearts are stone and mud, just as mine was once.

Oh, Love.
You healed me.
I came to You with broken parts.
I opened my heart to loving You.
Then You stopped me in my tracks,
opened me further, so nothing was hidden.
You dug into me, Love, You dug out the stones.
The things which weigh me.
 How can I tell them?
Give me the words!

Oh, Love.
My Love has never left me,
even when I could not speak HIS name.
My Love has never forsaken me,
even when I turned my face away.
My Love has never forgotten me,
even when my voice seems far away.
My Love is a King among all Loves,
The True One. The Only.
My Love I would give anything for them to know
You for a second as I have known You my whole life.
You gave everything for me, so that I could know You.
So that I could love You,
perhaps a splinter of the amount
You love me.

Oh, Love.
When I am with You, the stars are awake.
The earth moves and bounds like a young calve.
When You are with me, I swear the waters speak and trees sing.
Then all is still, all is quiet.
I turn, and there You are.

Oh, Love.
What I would give so that they knew You,
Spoke Your name with reverence.
With love.

PRAYER

We were a knot of hands that night.
A jumble of twisted arms and intwining fingers.
Our tears were lit by the fire around us,
Our smiles even more radiant.
We were a force to be reckoned with.
Thunder was under our feet.
Song was in our mouths.
Our laughter and sorrow too great to contain.
The light of our souls rolled into
One.
We were free.
Now our journey takes us far.
Wide are the miles between us.
This night alive in our hearts.
Our songs never far from the others.
We shake up the ground, the once firm foundations.
We cry out a tale of a love that never parts.
Never takes, never bolsters, never lives in pride.
Our hands now reach for you.
Will you join us?

ELOHIM

Dawn is a myriad of
Sound
Color
That we never hear elsewhere
I wait in dawn
In fields of rolling gold
For my Love
My Echad

He comes to me through shadows
He is light
No darkness touches Him
I cannot see His face
His form comes to me in dreams
I know Him
My Elohim

We dance through dawn and into day
There is no part to us
We are one
We are Echad
Elohim is my Love

You cannot take us apart
We are together in Spirit
Forever Always
Elohim and I

My eyes shine forever in His light
There is no end to His gentle touches
His graceful speeches and soft words

You may wage war
You may cross battle lines
You will not split my heart in two
Or four
Or seven

Because long ago I chose Love over Hate
There is no war that has not been won in my favor
For Elohim is my Love

Always
Forever
Mine
Just as I am His
There is no greater Love than this

Acknowledgements

It is only by the grace and glory of the Most High that this book is held in your hands. Where I have stumbled in my knowledge, a path has been made for me. I am truly grateful for all the people who have stepped forth to help. A deep and heartfelt thank you to Brandon Hallmark for an amazing job editing, and my superb sister of faith, Genevieve Kapsner for her beautiful design of the book itself. My thanks to everyone who cheered me on and pestered me (lovingly) toward publishing. Love to my family, who were there every step of the way and who continue to remind me that the craziness of life is an amazing thing.

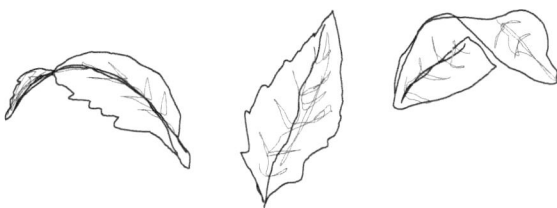

About the Author

Aryrejin El is a writer, dancer, artist, and teacher.
She has a great passion for life and helping others fulfill
their own lives and live as they were meant to.
You can find her online at www.Aryrejinel.com
On Instagram, or in the woods somewhere.

Until the Next Tale.